to

Eleanor

from

Leanne + Howard

Written and compiled by Lois Rock
Illustrations copyright © 2003, 2004 Alex Ayliffe
This edition copyright © 2012 Lion Hudson

Published by Lion Children's Books
an imprint of
Lion Hudson plc
Wilkinson House, Jordan Hill Road,
Oxford OX2 8DR, England
www.lionhudson.com/lionchildrens
ISBN 978 0 7459 6273 3

First edition 2012

Acknowledgments
All unattributed prayers by Lois Rock, copyright © Lion Hudson.
p.15: Attributed to John Chapman, planter of orchards
p.19: Julia Carney (1823–1908)
p.22: Mrs C. F. Alexander (1818–95)
p.24. Edith Rutter Leatham (1870–1939) (adapted)
p.28: From a New England sampler
p.29: Traditional
p.30: Traditional
The Lord's Prayer (on page 26) as it appears in *Common Worship: Services and Prayers for the
Church of England* (Church House Publishing, 2000) is copyright © The English Language
Liturgical Consultation and is reproduced by permission of the publisher.

A catalogue record for this book is available
from the British Library

Printed and bound in China, October 2014, LH17

my very first
Prayers
to Know by Heart

Words by Lois Rock
Pictures by Alex Ayliffe

LION
CHILDREN'S

The Maker God

Who made the sun?
Who made the day?
Who made the hours
for work and play?

God made them all,
God made them good,
God helps us live
the way we should.

Dearest God,
on this new day,
listen to me
as I pray.

Dearest God,
the day is new:
help me in
the things I do.

7

Here I am

God, look down from heaven:
Here on earth you'll see
Someone looking upwards –
That someone is me.

Bless my hair and bless my toes
Bless my ears and bless my nose
Bless my eyes and bless each hand
Bless the feet on which I stand
Bless my elbows, bless each knee:
God bless every part of me.

Good and kind

Open my eyes
So I can see
The ways I could
More useful be.

Give the strength
And heart and mind
To do the things
That are good and kind.

Home

Dear God, bless all my family,
as I tell you each name;
and please bless each one differently
for no one's quite the same.

Bless the window
Bless the door
Bless the ceiling
Bless the floor
Bless this place, which is our home
Bless us as we go and come.

Food

Let us take a moment
To thank God for our food,
For friends around the table
And everything that's good.

The Lord is good to me,
And so I thank the Lord
For giving me the things I need,
The sun, the rain, the appleseed.
The Lord is good to me.

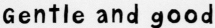

Gentle and good

May my hands be helping hands
For all that must be done
That fetch and carry, lift and hold
And make the hard jobs fun.

May my hands be clever hands
In all I make and do
With sand and dough and clay and things
With paper, paint and glue.

May my hands be gentle hands
And may I never dare
To poke and prod and hurt and harm
But touch with love and care.

17

Kind people

Thank you, dear God,
for the many kind people
who help us along on our way,
who smile when we're happy,
who care when we're tearful,
who keep us safe all through the day.

Little deeds of kindness,
Little words of love,
Help to make earth happy,
Like the heaven above.

out and about

For sun
and for showers,
for seeds
and for flowers,
we give you our thanks,
O God.

I love to have sand between my toes,
to watch the tide as it comes and goes,
to pick up shells and throw them away:
thank you, dear God, for my holiday.

Animals

All things bright and beautiful,
All creatures great and small,
All things wise and wonderful,
The Lord God made them all.

Multicoloured animals
With stripes and dots and patches:
God made each one different –
There isn't one that matches.

Little things

Dear Father God, please hear and bless
All animals and birds,
And guard with love and tenderness
Small things that have no words.

When little creatures die
And it's time to say goodbye
To a bright-eyed furry friend,
We know that God above
Will remember them with love:
A love that will never end.

The Lord's Prayer

Our Father in heaven,
hallowed be your name,
your kingdom come,
your will be done,
on earth as in heaven.
Give us today our daily bread.
Forgive us our sins
as we forgive those who sin against us.
Lead us not into temptation
but deliver us from evil.

For the kingdom, the power,
and the glory are yours
now and for ever.

Amen.

God bless

God bless all those that I love;
God bless all those that love me;
God bless all those that love those that I love,
And all those that love those that love me.

Now I lay me down to sleep,
I pray thee, Lord, thy child to keep;
Thy love to guard me through the night
And wake me in the morning light.

The moon shines bright,
The stars give light
Before the break of day;
God bless you all,
Both great and small,
And send a joyful day.